Inside Special Operations

ARMY RANGERS

Surveillance and Reconnaissance for the U.S. Army

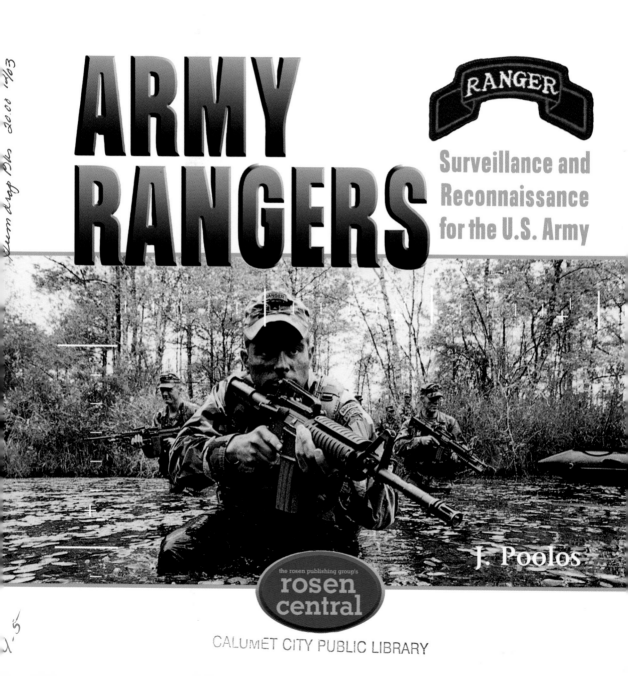

J. Poolos

the rosen publishing group's
rosen central

Published in 2003 by The Rosen Publishing Group, Inc.
29 East 21st Street, New York, NY 10010

First Edition

Library of Congress Cataloging-in-Publication Data
Poolos, J.
Army Rangers : surveillance and reconnaissance for the U.S. Army by J. Poolos—1st ed.
  p. cm.—(Inside special operations)
Summary: A look at an elite group of combat soldiers, the Army Rangers, including their purpose, history, missions, requirements, training, and equipment.
Includes bibliographical references and index.
ISBN 0-8239-3805-0 (library binding)
1. United States. Army——Commando troops—Juvenile literature.
[1.United States. Army—Commando troops. 2. Special forces (Military science)]
I. Title. II. Series.
UA34.R56 P66 2003
356'.163'0973—dc21

                                        2002008958

Manufactured in the United States of America

Contents

Outfitted in camouflage, U.S. Army Rangers ride special high-powered motorcycles rigged with automatic machine guns.

Introduction

The Army Ranger is an elite soldier, able to attack by land, air, or sea. As a combat soldier, he specializes in long-range surveillance and reconnaissance. He is also highly skilled at demolitions. As a teacher, he trains foreign armed forces and special-interest factions in their home countries. He must be in top physical condition. He must be an expert in firearms and Ranger tactics. And he must be able to both lead and follow.

Rangers can be deployed by Special Operations Forces (SOF) or by the army command. They have seen action in conflicts from colonial times to the recent situation in Afghanistan. They have fought and died in America's most important battles, often leading army infantry units into large-scale engagements with the enemy. They have also played a major role in hostage rescue and in training friendly forces.

In this book you will find everything you need to know about the U.S. Army Rangers. You will learn about the origins of the Rangers and their role in historic wars and missions. You will learn about the influential leaders who shaped the Rangers into the force they are now. You will also learn about the weapons and gear each Ranger uses and about the rigorous training each must endure to earn the coveted Ranger tab. Finally, you will learn about the Ranger "code," areas of specialization, and what it takes to be a Ranger.

"Rangers lead the way!"

History: 1. 1670–1950

When you think of the U.S. Army Rangers, you think of well-trained men who can take care of themselves in the most difficult situations—men who can move over rugged terrain, silent and unseen, men who can live off the land and, if necessary, shoot straight. With this image in mind, the modern Rangers' origins should come as no surprise.

The Pre-Revolutionary Rangers

The Rangers first operated in the American frontier in the early 1670s during the conflict with Native American Indians known as King Philip's War. At that time, soldiers fighting American Indians found that traditional European tactics were no match for the fighting style of their foes or the rugged terrain on which they fought. The Native American warrior had the distinct advantage of being able to use stealth to spy on his enemy and to conduct surprise raids at the right moment.

In order to survive, new strategies were required. Imitating the Indians' reconnaissance techniques, frontiersmen began sending out small groups of men to scout the countryside for signs of enemy movement and, if necessary, to provide early warning to neighboring settlements. These Rangers, given the name because they "ranged" over the land, began to use more Indian tactics to great success. These tactics included long-range travel on foot and horseback, as well as over-land and over-water raids.

In 1756, Major Robert Rogers began to lead American colonists to fight on the British side during the French and Indian War. He drew up a list of rules by which Rangers continue to abide today. These rules were the focus of a training program that was designed to teach the men how to think creatively to catch the enemy off guard and how to prepare for the attack. For instance, during the winter of 1758, when other fighting units were hunkered down in their winter camps, Rogers's Rangers sent scouts to locate the French and the Indians. Then they devised plans and

This painting depicts the savage "Battle on Snowshoes" at what is now known as Rogers Rock. On March 13, 1758, Rogers and 180 of his Rangers were outnumbered by a group of French, Canadians, and Indians. After fighting admirably in the frozen woods, 125 Rangers were killed.

innovative techniques to allow them to reach and attack the enemy by surprise. Rangers used snowshoes, sleds, and ice skates to take the fight to the French and the Indians.

The Rangers in the Revolutionary War

For the next ten years, the Rangers continued to defend colonists against occasional Indian attacks. But soon there was a greater need. In 1775, with the colonies on the verge of a war of independence with Great Britain, the Continental Congress commissioned ten companies of "expert riflemen" from Maryland, Pennsylvania, and Virginia. This core group of men, led by Dan Morgan, became the American Revolution's first corps of Rangers.

Another group of men was led by Francis Marion. Marion was known as the Swamp Fox because he had the reputation for outwitting the British, then sneaking off to hide in the woods and swamps of South Carolina. He helped to defend the important port of Charleston and disrupt enemy communications.

The Texas Rangers

Shortly after the revolt of 1836, the Republic of Texas formed several small companies of horsemen who became the Texas Rangers. These Rangers responded to the volatile political situation that prevailed at the time. They were assigned to travel swiftly by horse, protecting the frontier against Indians, Mexican bandits, and even Mexican soldiers. When the conflict with Mexico reached its height, the Mexican War began, and the Rangers were ready. Colonel John C. Hayes was put in charge of a cavalry regiment of Rangers. These men were used primarily as scouts and cavalrymen, but they were known for their sharpshooting and high level of discipline.

The Rangers in the Civil War

In 1862 the Confederate colonel John S. Mosby was put in charge of a three-man scouting unit. This unit was assigned to operate behind the Union lines on the south side of the Potomac River. By 1865, Mosby's Rangers consisted of eight companies. Mosby's great success came from using a tactic that forced the enemy to guard many positions at once. His strategy was to move small parties of men, usually between twenty and fifty, into a location where they could aggressively attack an enemy position, then quickly withdraw. Various parties would attack several locations, forcing the enemy to be on guard at each point of attack, wondering where the next attack would come. Mosby would then send out small reconnaissance teams to identify a weak point in the enemy defense. Once he got the report, his men focused an attack on the weak point. This technique

Colonel John Singleton Mosby (1833–1916) was an aggressive strategist in the Civil War. He is often credited with helping fend off a Union victory in the fall of 1864.

was productive in two ways. One, it won battles. And two, it terrorized the Rangers' enemies, confusing them and forcing them to second-guess their strategies.

World War II

By the time America had entered into the second great war of the twentieth century, the Ranger concept was well defined. The U.S. Army had spent years refining the purpose of the Ranger, the types of missions to which he would be best suited, and the training that was necessary to make him most effective.

Major General Lucian K. Truscott (1895–1965) studies a map with Lieutenant General Omar N. Bradley during World War II. Truscott enlisted in the army in World War I and had a long, distinguished military career.

It wasn't long after the Japanese bombed Pearl Harbor on December 7, 1941, that a U.S. Army liaison with the British General Staff had the idea that the Allied forces would need specialized scouting and reconnaissance units. According to the Army

Rangers Web site (http://www.ranger.org), Major General Lucian K. Truscott proposed to General George Marshall that "we undertake immediately an American unit along the lines of the British Commandos." Thus, the 1st U.S. Army Ranger Battalion was authorized.

Truscott chose the name "Rangers," because it was "fitting that the organization that was destined to be the first of the American Ground Forces to battle Germans on the European continent should be called Rangers in compliment to those in

Led by Captain William Darby, the 1st Ranger Battalion stormed Omaha Beach, France, clearing the area for Allied troops to fight the Germans. Rangers' willingness to enter a situation first no matter how dangerous is stated in their motto: "Rangers lead the way!"

American history who exemplified the high standards of courage, initiative, determination and ruggedness, fighting ability and achievement."

Truscott and Major General Russell P. Hartle, who commanded all army forces in Northern Ireland, recommended Captain William Orlando Darby to head up the first battalion. On June 19, 1942, the 1st Ranger Battalion was activated, marking the birth of the modern Ranger.

This battalion spearheaded the North African invasion, which cleared the way for General George S. Patton's forces. Later Darby led Rangers during the Omaha Beach, France, landings on D-Day. These Rangers faced a barrage of artillery and machine-gun fire. They fought for two straight days and nights to eliminate gunneries and clear the way for Allied fleets to move closer to the shore, where they could fire their massive guns at the beachhead. Additional Ranger battalions stormed the beach, suffering as much as 50 percent casualties as they scaled the sheer cliffs to take out the fortified German guns. Here the motto of the 75th Ranger Regiment was born, when General Norman D. Cota gave the order, "Rangers lead the way!"

Ranger battalions played a major role in the European theater, participating in the infamous Battle of the Bulge, as well as major conflicts in France and Italy. But they also drew fire in the Pacific. It was here that the Rangers performed what is described on the Ranger Web site as the "greatest and most daring raid in American military history." On January 30, 1944, C Company marched thirty miles behind enemy lines and liberated over 500 POWs (prisoners of war)—all survivors of the infamous Bataan Death March. The Rangers, many carrying sickly prisoners on their backs, eluded several Japanese regiments as they marched toward the safety of the American line the next day. It was truly a heroic moment for the Rangers, and a sign of things to come for the next fifty years.

Korea

The Korean conflict, which began in 1950, called for an even more modern Ranger. As a result, a new training program

was instituted in Fort Benning, Georgia. The training consisted of ground and amphibious assault, as well as airborne assault with an emphasis on low-level night jumps. Trainees conducted exercises in demolitions, sabotage, close combat, and the use of foreign maps. They also mastered American small arms and artillery, as well as enemy small arms. In addition to being highly skilled in a variety of combat methods, the "new" Ranger was put through a rigorous physical regimen that included long night marches and extended periods in the field.

On December 17, 1950, the 1st Ranger Infantry Company (Airborne) arrived in Korea, ready for action. There it was attached to the 2nd Infantry Division. Additional companies were attached to infantry divisions at the rate of a single 112-Ranger company per one 18,000-man infantry division. These Ranger companies led the infantry divisions, performing scouting, patrol, raid, ambush, and assault actions with remarkable success. They attacked by air, land, and water, and were awarded various distinguished commendations. Their heroic actions and outstanding results drew the attention of superior commanders, whose successors continue to use the Fort Benning training program today.

2. Famous Ranger Leaders

The success of every military mission depends on the effectiveness of its leaders. The men who led the Rangers into combat were a special breed. More than most other leaders, they quickly discarded tactics that did not produce results. And they invented their own strategies and techniques. The incredible men described in this chapter played important roles in shaping today's Rangers.

Major Robert Rogers

In 1756, the model for today's Rangers began to take shape. It all began when Major Robert Rogers, a long-time soldier, recruited nine companies of American colonists to fight on the British side during the French and Indian War. Although the techniques of the frontiersman had been used for the first time nearly 100 years earlier, Rogers was the first to marry these techniques to a formal military structure. In fact, Rogers was so influential that today's U.S. Army Rangers still use his list of twenty-eight rules as guiding principles.

Rogers's most famous raid was directed against the Abenaki Indians, a tribe known for their fierce, relentless fighting. The Abenaki settlement was about 400 miles away from Rogers's base camp, Crown Point, on Lake Champlain in New York. Rogers set out with 200 Rangers by land and boat. They covered the distance in sixty days, moving deep into enemy territory. When the time was right they attacked, killing several hundred Indians and wiping out the settlement. The raid was a success, and the British could move forward without fear of

Robert Rogers (1731–1795) was a frontiersman famous for leading Rangers in the French and Indian War.

attack from the Abenaki. Rogers prided himself on the dedication and effectiveness of his men: While other units were hindered by weather and terrain, his Rangers got the job done.

Francis Marion, the Swamp Fox

The most famous of the Revolutionary War's guerrilla fighters was a man called the Swamp Fox. A farmer from South Carolina, Francis Marion learned the tactics of surprise attacks from the Cherokees. He also learned how to use the forests and swamps of his native state for cover. Marion made a name for the Rangers when he defended the strategic port of Charleston from the British navy. As the first of the fleet drew within range of his island fort, the crafty Swamp Fox used a defense of strike and retreat, confusing the British command and crippling some fifty ships.

The defense of Charleston was the first important victory for the colonists. Later, when the British sent reinforcements too strong for the colonists to defeat, Marion and his men fled to the swamps. There Marion formed Marion's Brigade, a ragtag group of men who had left their families and their farms to fight for their country. The Swamp Fox and his brigade descended on British camps for the entire war, never receiving pay or ammunition from the Continental Army. They disrupted British communications and terrorized British loyalists.

Standing Orders, Rogers's Rangers

- Don't forget nothing.

- Have your musket clean as a whistle, hatchet scoured, sixty rounds powder and ball, and be ready to march at a minute's warning.

- When you're on the march, act the way you would if you was sneaking up on a deer. See the enemy first.

- Tell the truth about what you see and what you do. There is an army depending on us for correct information. You can lie all you please when you tell other folks about the Rangers, but don't never lie to a Ranger or officer.

- Don't never take a chance you don't have to.

- When we're on the march we march single file, far enough apart so one shot can't go through two men.

- If we strike swamps, or soft ground, we spread out abreast, so it's hard to track us.

- When we march, we keep moving till dark, so as to give the enemy the least possible chance at us.

- When we camp, half the party stays awake while the other half sleeps.

- If we take prisoners, we keep 'em separate till we have had time to examine them, so they can't cook up a story between 'em.

- Don't ever march home the same way. Take a different route so you won't be ambushed.

- No matter whether we travel in big parties or little ones, each party has to keep a scout 20 yards ahead, 20 yards on each flank, and 20 yards in the rear so the main body can't be surprised and wiped out.

- Every night you'll be told where to meet if surrounded by a superior force.

- Don't sit down to eat without posting sentries.

- Don't sleep beyond dawn. Dawn's when the French and Indians attack.

- Don't cross a river by a regular ford.

- If somebody's trailing you, make a circle, come back onto your own tracks, and ambush the folks that aim to ambush you.

- Don't stand up when the enemy's coming against you. Kneel down, lie down, hide behind a tree.

- Let the enemy come till he's almost close enough to touch, then let him have it and jump out and finish him up with your hatchet.

—Major Robert Rogers, 1759
from the United States Army Infantry School
Ranger Handbook

William Orlando Darby

A graduate of the West Point military academy, William Orlando Darby had amphibious training, which made him an attractive candidate for the position of Ranger commander during World War II. On June 19, 1942, the 1st Ranger Battalion was activated. This group of some 600 men attended the Commando Training Center in Achnacarry, Scotland. There they learned the tactics used by the British commandos. The skills they mastered would prove invaluable to the Allies in the long, brutal encounter that was World War II.

Lieutenant Colonel William Darby *(right)* with a French field soldier in North Africa during World War II. Darby was killed in action just days before the end of the war.

When their training was finished, the 1st Ranger Battalion spearheaded the North African invasion. A smaller group landed at the port of Arzew, Algeria, in the dead of night. Once they secured the area, they took out two gun batteries and cleared the way for the infantry to capture the city of Oran. Several encounters followed. Rangers won them all.

The high point of the Rangers' North African campaign came on March 31, 1943, when the 1st Ranger Battalion marched twelve miles by night and captured the port of El Guettar, Tunisia. The soldiers fought for the remainder of the night, then launched a surprise attack on the unsuspecting Italians, capturing 200 prisoners and clearing the way for General Patton's forces to launch the Allied invasion of Africa. Following this raid, the battalion was awarded its first Presidential Citation.

Based on the success of the 1st Ranger Battalion, the U.S. Army activated and trained two additional battalions, all of which fell under Darby's general command and were known as Darby's Rangers. These units played a major role in the campaigns in Italy and won numerous high-level citations for their bravery and valor. Eventually, elements of the 82nd Airborne Division, artillery, and chemical warfare units fell under Darby's command. Darby himself was promoted to colonel.

Meanwhile, an additional Ranger battalion spearheaded the Omaha Beach landings. These Rangers helped the Allies triumph in what was considered by many to be a battle impossible to win.

Frank D. Merrill

During the Quebec Conference of 1943, American president Franklin D. Roosevelt and British prime minister Winston

Churchill came up with the idea to create an American ground unit that would penetrate deep behind enemy lines in Burma (now called Myanmar) and attack veteran Japanese troops. The 5307th Composite Unit became known as Merrill's Marauders, after its leader, Frank D. Merrill. After secret training in the jungles of India, the Marauders traveled to northwestern Burma and fought their way through 1,000 miles of thick jungles and over mountains from Hukawng Valley to Myitkyina and the Irrawaddy River. They met the Japanese in five major and approximately thirty minor engagements, often outnumbered by superior forces. Along the way, they played havoc on enemy communications and supply lines, contributing to the overall effort of the U.S. Army. This was the last victory for the Marauders. Of the 3,000 original volunteers, 2,400 were killed, wounded, or suffered disease during the extremely hazardous ninety-day campaign. Although these men were not officially designated as Rangers, they used standard Ranger tactics.

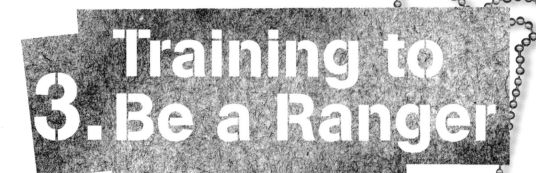

3. Training to Be a Ranger

It goes without saying that all U.S. Army Rangers are expected to be in top physical condition. But Rangers must possess a number of other qualities, including the ability to memorize data, to assess a situation, and to apply knowledge to make the best decision. Many of these skills are honed, and even taught, in Ranger school. But to survive there, candidates must bring a desire to succeed and the determination to push beyond extreme physical discomfort. Many are accepted to Ranger school; few will become Rangers. This chapter outlines the basic preliminary training a candidate must undergo

Recruits take lessons in rope climbing and descending during the Ranger course. Rope work is a skill that is used when Rangers are called on to descend from a helicopter.

before he becomes one of the select few U.S. Army Rangers.

The Ranger course is made up of sixty-one days packed with education and challenging training exercises. On average, the candidate partakes in more than nineteen hours of training each day, seven days a week. The course is made up of three phases, each tailored to a different physical location suitable for emphasizing specific aspects of close-range combat.

The overall purpose of the course, according to the Ranger course pamphlet, is to "teach and develop combat arms functional skills relevant to fighting close combat, direct fire battle." The typical exercise is designed to allow each student to learn while under pressure. Usually this means solving difficult problems in stressful situations, such as simulated combat conditions.

Throughout the course students act as both leaders and followers. They learn the most current fighting methods, often referred to as tactical doctrine. Emphasis is placed on planning and conducting a variety of missions, including airborne, waterborne, air assault, and operations with different sized teams.

As if the long hours and hard training were not enough stress, students are exposed to conditions that in some cases are designed to be even more difficult than those they can expect to see in actual combat. These conditions include fatigue and hunger. Students are expected to rise above the physical discomfort and demonstrate a calm confidence while making intelligent decisions. By the end of the course, students will have practical experience planning and executing missions in near-combat situations. They will have been evaluated in a series of field exercises conducted at night in various weather conditions.

During urban attack training, members of the U.S. Army Rangers carefully enter a building and secure its interior.

The Benning Phase

The Benning Phase is the first of the three phases that make up Ranger school. It is twenty days in length and is conducted by the 4th Battalion, Ranger Training Brigade at Fort Benning, Georgia. The purpose of this phase is to assess and develop the military skills, physical and mental endurance, and confidence typically required of a soldier in combat conditions. Students must learn how to take care of themselves and other students, as well as keep their equipment in excellent working order.

Benning Phase Physical Tests Part One

- 49 push-ups
- 59 sit-ups
- 2-mile run in 15 minutes or less
- 6 chin-ups
- combat water survival test
- 5-mile run
- 3-mile run with an obstacle course

- 16-mile march
- land navigation tests during night and day
- rifle, bayonet, and hand-to-hand combat
- water confidence test
- terrain association
- demolitions
- airborne refresher jump

The Benning Phase is primarily a test of physical and mental endurance, but it is the foundation of Ranger school. Students who cannot keep up during the exercises in this phase will have difficulty completing the course.

The Benning Phase is conducted in two parts. The first part is made up of physical and mental exercises, which are designed to test endurance and toughness. Once students complete the first part of the phase, they advance to the second part, where the emphasis shifts to instruction in patrol operations. Students receive fieldcraft training (how to survive in the field, including camouflage; radio operations; and the use of maps, compasses, and a global positioning system), run the infamous Darby Queen Obstacle Course, and master the fundamentals of patrolling, including knowledge of response protocol and communications. They also learn about how to conduct various patrols, such as reconnaissance and ambush. The final portion of the course requires the students to demonstrate their knowledge through a number of tactical patrols, or field exercises. The end goal is for the student to gain proficiency and confidence to partake in the next phase of the school.

Mountain Phase

The Mountain Phase is twenty-one days long. It is conducted by the 5th Battalion, Ranger Training Brigade at Camp Frank D. Merrill, Dahlonega, Georgia. As the name implies, the

Mountain Phase centers on military mountaineering tasks. Students learn how to employ a squad and platoon for combat patrol operations. An emphasis is put on planning, preparation, and execution of various combat missions. Here the student faces "rugged terrain, severe hunger, mental and physical fatigue, and the emotional stress . . . that affords him the opportunity to gauge his own capabilities and limitations," according to the Ranger course pamphlet. A major focus is mountaineering, and students learn about knots, anchor points, rope management, and the basics of climbing and rappelling. Students must then complete a 200-foot night rappel at Yonah Mountain to continue the course.

The Mountain Phase trains Ranger students to navigate rough terrain. Here, a soldier climbs cliffs similar to those in Afghanistan.

Those who pass the test move on to more sophisticated exercises and tests. These include four- and five-day treks. Along the way, students ambush vehicles and raid communication sites. It is nonstop, grueling work. They must cross rivers, move over mountains, and conduct air assaults, followed by a ten-mile foot march to a target. The course stresses the students' commitment, as anyone may be singled out at any time to lead a squad of hungry and exhausted students through the next test.

Ranger training is so grueling that many recruits are pushed beyond their physical and mental limits. Above, a Ranger rests in the mud during his training at Hunter Army Base in Georgia.

Florida Phase

The Florida Phase is eighteen days in length and is conducted by the 6th Battalion, Ranger Training Brigade, at Camp James E. Rudder at Elgin Air Force Base, Florida. The focus shifts to the coordination of airborne, small-boat, and ship-to-shore assaults. By this time, most students have moved beyond their former limits for fatigue. In this sense, they are exploring new territory, and every day they survive is a victory. Students must reach deep to succeed in these grueling group exercises, which are conducted in a swamp environment.

Ranger Creed

Recognizing that I volunteered as a Ranger, fully knowing the hazards of my chosen profession, I will always endeavor to uphold the prestige, honor, and high "esprit de corps" of the Rangers.

Acknowledging the fact that a Ranger is a more elite soldier who arrives at the cutting edge of battle by land, sea, or air, I accept the fact that as a Ranger my country expects me to move further, faster and fight harder than any other soldier.

Never shall I fail my comrades. I will always keep myself mentally alert, physically strong and morally straight and I will shoulder more than my share of the task whatever it may be. One hundred percent and then some.

Gallantly will I show the world that I am a specially selected and well-trained soldier. My courtesy to superior officers, neatness of dress and care of equipment shall set the example for others to follow.

Energetically will I meet the enemies of my country. I shall defeat them on the field of battle for I am better trained and will fight with all my might. Surrender is not a Ranger word. I will never leave a fallen comrade to fall into the hands of the enemy and under no circumstances will I ever embarrass my country.

Readily will I display the intestinal fortitude required to fight on to the Ranger objective and complete the mission, though I be the lone survivor. RANGERS LEAD THE WAY!

This phase of the training emphasizes sustained scenarios in which students must select and apply the techniques they have learned in the first two phases of the course. They receive additional training in small-boat operations, stream-crossing techniques, and jungle survival. The final ten-day test is fast-paced and highly stressful. After completing the Florida Phase students perform an airborne insertion back into Fort Benning.

Having reached the end of the course, the student has become a hardened soldier, confident he can conduct himself and lead others in a wide variety of extreme conditions. He has demonstrated that he can prepare for and execute small-unit night operations, low-altitude mountaineering, and infiltration/exfiltration via land, air, and sea. Having passed the Ranger school, he is fully authorized to wear the Ranger tab. For a select few, this training is a base for additional training in other Special Forces. In any case, those who pass Ranger school have achieved a level of accomplishment most can only dream of.

4. A Ranger's Equipment

Special Forces require special tools, and the Rangers are no exception. Most Ranger missions are much more low-key, and often secretive, than the typical army mission. A Ranger unit rarely carries more than what it needs to accomplish a given objective. Rangers have been trained to rely on their smarts more than on force. They may sacrifice the necessary ammunition if the resulting lighter load means they will increase their ability to maneuver out of trouble if necessary.

Every Ranger chooses his equipment carefully, based on the mission.

The wrong choice could mean the difference between life and death. Following is a list of the basic equipment and weapons from which a Ranger may assemble a "load."

Clothing and Body Armor

With a variety of gear available to them, the Rangers' rule is wear what works. In a mission calling for infiltration into an urban setting, a Ranger may wear street clothes. In a reconnaissance situation, Rangers may wear uniforms with one of a number of different camouflage patterns. Each Ranger is issued a Kevlar helmet and a flak jacket for protection against small-arms fire.

For some missions, a Ranger must carry a load that exceeds his body weight. This load may include explosives and ammunition for specialized weapons, such as grenade launchers or land mines. The standard pack is the all-purpose lightweight individual carrying equipment system (ALICE), which is a large pack on an aluminum frame.

Weapons

A Ranger would select a few of the following weapons to add to his load, being careful not to weigh himself down.

M4 5.6mm carbine Based on the M16 combat rifle, which is the most common rifle in today's military, the M4 is a lightweight version designed especially for Special Forces. It was first used in the Vietnam War. The M4 uses NATO-compatible 5.6mm ammunition. But it is the foundation of a system in which other attachments can change the gun into a grenade launcher, a sighting device, or a low-light/thermal-imaging system.

MP-5 9mm submachine gun The MP-5 is a close-range weapon that fires standard NATO 9mm pistol ammunition. It features both semiautomatic and fully automatic modes. Because the weapon can fire a lot of rounds accurately in a short burst, it is used primarily in close-combat situations, such as urban raids.

M24 sniper rifle Although the Rangers don't train to be the most effective snipers in the U.S. armed forces, many receive training in sniper tactics. The M24 has a range of 500 yards and is equipped with a 10 x 24 Leupold M3 Ultra scope. It was first issued in 1988.

M249 5.56mm squad automatic weapon (SAW) The M249 is the standard light machine gun in the U.S. military. It is based on a Belgian design. It fires the same ammunition as the M4 rifle, either from a belt or a thirty-round magazine. It can be mounted on a tripod or a vehicle. Its main advantage is that it can be operated by a single soldier.

M9 Beretta 9mm pistol   Because he operates in close-combat situations or under cover, a Ranger may rely on his pistol more than any other weapon. The M9 Beretta fires from a fifteen-round magazine. It is a semiautomatic pistol, which means it fires single rounds without recocking.

M240G 7.62mm light machine gun   The M240G is used by Rangers to defend pre-established bases or points of interest. It fires a heavier cartridge than the standard 5.56 round, so it has more power and penetrating ability. It also has a greater range.

M203 40mm grenade launcher   The M203 is an attachment that clips under the barrel of a rifle.

An Army Ranger lines up a target using the telescopic sight attached to an M240 machine gun. Rangers are trained to use many different types of weapons.

It fires grenades accurately up to 330 feet. Its primary advantage is that it adds the power of a grenade launcher in a package weighing less than four pounds while allowing the Ranger to retain his rifle.

Mk. 19 40mm grenade launcher Like the M240G, the Mk. 19 grenade launcher is used primarily to defend points of interest. It was originally developed by the navy to mount on patrol boats. The Mk. 19 is a fully automatic grenade launcher, able to fire sixty grenades per minute.

Hand grenades Rangers may carry any of the roughly twelve types of hand grenades used in today's Special Forces. The most common is the M67 fragmentation grenade. Others include smoke, tear gas, and concussion. Rangers commonly use smoke grenades to signal pickup points as well as targets.

Army Rangers must know how and when to use many types of grenades. Above, an antipersonnel fragmentation grenade.

Multi-purpose infantry munition Rangers are also trained to use rocket launchers, antiarmor missiles, and other heavy weapons systems. These are used primarily to disable tanks, armored vehicles, and, in some cases, aircraft. Some of these weapons consist of guided missiles and disposable firing tubes. They may have a range from 50 to 1,600 feet, making them ideal for urban encounters.

Javelin antitank missile The Javelin antitank missile can lock onto a target's thermal signature from 8,200 feet. Common targets include tanks, armored vehicles, buildings and bunkers, and low-flying aircraft. The Rangers may use a weapon like this on rare occasions because it takes two soldiers to carry it.

Foreign weapons Rangers are trained in the use of foreign-made weapons systems for a number of reasons. Often when they go into a country to train soldiers, they must demonstrate their expertise with a weapon in order to gain the confidence of the men they will train. They must be able to demonstrate excellent marksmanship as well as the ability to disassemble and clean a weapon. It is also useful to know the capabilities of the weapons that may be used against them in combat.

Explosives Rangers are skilled at using a variety of explosives. The most common explosive is C4, sometimes called plastique. C4 has the texture of clay and can be molded into various shapes. Rangers use explosives to destroy bridges and other strategic structures. For lighter jobs, such as breaking through heavy doors, Rangers employ detonation cord, which is a synthetic rope made partly of explosives.

Navigation

Because they may be traveling across unknown territory under conditions of darkness or limited visibility, Rangers need sophisticated tools for finding their way.

Global positioning system Twenty-four satellites orbit Earth sending signals to global positioning receivers, such as those seen in many of today's high-end automobiles. Ranger teams carry these receivers, too. The standard receiver for Rangers is the Rockwell Collins AN/PSN-11 portable lightweight receiver. It is accurate to within twenty feet (around six meters) and can be used for many purposes, including guiding missiles to targets. But Rangers use GPS primarily to navigate in the wilderness.

Compass Rangers have always prided themselves on their ability to navigate sparsely populated woods, swamps, and

Army Rangers use a laptop computer to communicate with soldiers in the field and at headquarters. The computer features a collapsible antenna and a wireless connection that operates using a satellite. Having access to the latest technology gives soldiers an edge on their missions.

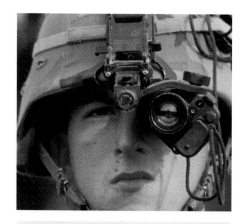

Night vision goggles enable Army Rangers to assess terrain and monitor an enemy's movements in darkness.

mountainous regions. Their specialty is over-land navigation. For years their primary tools have been compasses and maps. Should a global positioning system fail, the Ranger has nothing to rely on but the traditional tools of his trade. For this reason, each Ranger receives extensive training and is thoroughly tested in the use of a compass for navigation.

Night vision goggles Modern night vision goggles can be worn on the helmet, or they can be hand-held devices similar to binoculars. The standard-issue night vision goggle for the Special Forces is the PVS-7D. It magnifies millions of times what little light there is at night, whether it be from stars or from distant streetlights. The result is a fairly clear picture, although all objects appear green.

5. Rangers in Combat

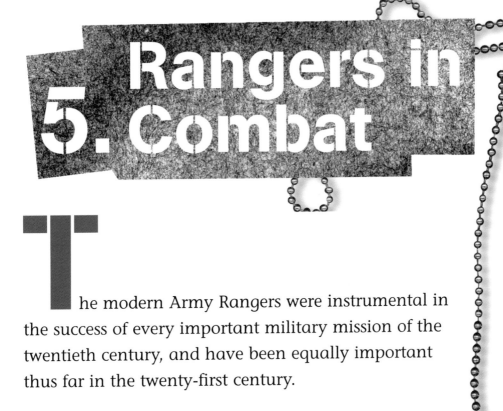

The modern Army Rangers were instrumental in the success of every important military mission of the twentieth century, and have been equally important thus far in the twenty-first century.

World War II, D-Day

In June 1944, the German army recognized the threat of an invasion of the French side of the English Channel, which Germany occupied. They built a steel wall of defense, fortified with 58 divisions, including 2,000 tanks. Allied commanders called on Special Forces to soften up the defenses before regulars

After storming Omaha Beach on D-Day, Army Rangers climbed a rope ladder to sneak up on and attack a German gun crew stationed at the top of a cliff, as shown in the reenactment above. By wiping out the crew, the Rangers cleared the way for Allied troops to advance.

landed to carry on the fight. These included the 2nd and 5th Ranger Battalions, the 82nd Airborne, the 101st Airborne, and the Screaming Eagles, among others.

On the morning of June 6, 1944, the 2nd and 5th Ranger Battalions landed on the beaches of Normandy. They were divided into three groups, each with its own objective. Group A was assigned to scale the sheer cliffs at Pointe-du-Hoc and destroy six large-caliber guns. These guns were secured in bunkers and reinforced by numerous German troops. If the Rangers failed, the Germans would use the guns to wreak havoc on the Allied troops that would soon land.

Group B was assigned to wait offshore for thirty minutes

before coming to the aid of Group A. Group C was assigned to scale the cliffs at nearby Pointe-et-Raz-de-la-Percee, where they were to take out mortar emplacements.

When the Rangers of Group A reached the top of the cliffs through heavy enemy fire, they learned that the guns had been moved. But they found them unguarded about a mile away. The Rangers attached grenades to the guns, rendering them useless. Meanwhile, Group B landed in a hail of heavy fire. As Patrick O'Donnel describes in his book *Beyond Valor*, "[a]rtillery, mortar, and machine gun fire ripped through the bodies of the Rangers as they made their way across the Charlie sector [a section of the beach under heavy fire] of Omaha Beach to the 90-foot cliffs." Group B used bayonets to fight their way to the top of the cliff, where they secured the position.

The three groups met at a rendezvous point. For the next three days they held off the enemy. When the Rangers ran out of ammunition, they fought the Germans with their own weapons, which the Rangers had confiscated or found. For their heroics they were awarded a Presidential Citation.

Operation Urgent Fury, Grenada

In October 1983, the Rangers got the call to rescue American hostages on the tiny island of Grenada in the West Indies.

Because of a government takeover by a Cuban communist group called the People's Revolutionary Army, all Americans living on the island were forbidden to leave. The Rangers' mission was to protect the lives of American citizens and to restore democracy to Grenada. The American invasion of Grenada was called Operation Urgent Fury. It had three objectives: Rangers would secure the airport at Point Salinas, rescue the American students at the True Blue Medical campus, and capture the Cubans' army camp.

At about 6:00 AM the Rangers parachuted in to the airfield with a low-level drop, and once on the ground began clearing the runways. When American planes carrying supplies could land safely, the Rangers moved off toward the True Blue Medical campus. By 10:00 AM the 2nd Platoon, A Company, had rescued the students and moved them to the airfield, where they boarded a plane and flew back to the United States.

Before the Rangers had set out to capture the Cubans' army camp, the Cubans attacked them with three armored personnel carriers. These were easily defeated, with many of the Cuban soldiers killed. The next day the Rangers attacked the Cuban army barracks at Calivigny. But three MH-60 Blackhawk helicopters crashed while trying to land. Three Rangers were killed in the encounter. The Rangers discovered that the Cubans had deserted the barracks. All the Rangers could do was wait for morning, when they were airlifted back home.

Operation Just Cause, Panama

On December 20, 1989, the 75th Ranger Regiment was called upon to perform a mission considered of the highest importance to American interests. In Operation Just Cause, 2,000 soldiers participated in the invasion of Panama with the goal of restoring democracy. The main objectives were Torrijos-Tocumen International Airport, Rio Hato Military Airfield, and Panamanian president Manuel Noriega's beach house. The absolute objectives were to remove Noriega from power and to neutralize the Panamanian Defense Force.

Rangers from 1/75, C Company 3/75, and Team Gold were inserted into Torrijos-Tocumen International Airport via low-level parachute jumps. Meanwhile, 2/75, A and B 3/75, and Team Black jumped into Rio Hato Military Airfield. These Rangers were hit with heavy antiaircraft fire during the insertion process. Within two hours Rio Hato was secure. The Americans then used the airport to fly in transport aircraft with supplies, including food, ammunition, and additional weapons.

After they secured the airports, the Rangers moved out and fought Panamanian special forces, known as the Mountain Troops. Rangers went house to house where the soldiers lived with their families. (Many of the Mountain Troops were captured while trying to shave off their distinctive beards.)

At this time President Noriega took refuge in the Vatican Embassy. Rangers guarded the embassy to see that no damage was done. They also took many photographs of Panamanian buildings, businesses, and military interests to show that they had not needlessly destroyed property.

Five Rangers were killed in action. Forty-two were wounded. Yet the Rangers took 1,014 prisoners of war. The Rangers accomplished their mission and returned home January 7, 1990.

Task Force Ranger, Somalia

Task Force Ranger arrived in Somalia, Africa, in August 1993. Their mission was to support United Nations operations and to capture General Mohammed Farah Aideed and his key lieutenants. During the month of September the Rangers staged six missions in the city of Mogadishu. But they were unable to locate Aideed.

On October 3, Task Force Ranger launched its seventh mission, to attack Aideed's stronghold. During the fight the Rangers were under a hail of enemy fire. Then an MH-60 Blackhawk helicopter was shot down several blocks from Aideed's compound. Immediately an MH-6 assault helicopter and another MH-60 Blackhawk carrying a fifteen-man rescue team were sent to the scene. As the rescue team was unloading, a second Blackhawk was shot down about a mile from the first. A mob overran the second crash, killing everyone but the pilot, whom they took prisoner.

Back at the first crash site, the Task Force Rangers and rescue team held off aggressive Somali forces while they tended to the wounded and tried to free the pilot's body from the wrecked helicopter. Meanwhile, two convoys of trucks and soldiers were trying to make their way through the narrow, winding streets to help. But roadblocks and heavy fire forced them to retreat. That night, the Task Force Rangers at the first fallen chopper were resupplied, and they continued to work to free the pilot's body. Finally, on the morning of October 4, reinforcements arrived to help. At dawn, they loaded the casualties into armored personnel carriers and moved out. Rangers on foot used the vehicles for cover. The "Mogadishu Mile" was supported by heavy air cover. Eventually, the Rangers and the reinforcements arrived at a secure stadium, where the wounded were treated.

Soldiers stand in front of two Blackhawk helicopters. The tragedy in Somalia is the subject of the book *Black Hawk Down.*

By the end of the mission, seventeen Rangers had lost their lives and 106 were wounded in some of the most difficult fighting in Ranger history.

Operation Enduring Freedom, Afghanistan

After the September 11, 2001, terrorist attacks on America, President George W. Bush launched Operation Enduring Freedom. The objective was to capture or kill Osama bin Laden and important members of Al Qaeda, bin Laden's terrorist organization. Another mission objective was to remove the Taliban regime, which supported bin Laden, from leadership in Afghanistan.

On October 19, 2001, about 100 Rangers parachuted into two locations in Afghanistan. Once on the ground, they gathered intelligence and destroyed weapons caches outside the city of Khandahar and near a small airfield to the south.

In December 2001 and January 2002, Rangers were assigned the task of flushing out bin Laden from his hiding place. They searched a vast network of caves where Al Qaeda forces had been seen. Much of the information regarding Rangers in Operation Enduring Freedom remains classified. As of this printing, the Rangers are still trying to locate and capture bin Laden.

6. The Rangers Today

In 1973, in response to the attack called the Yom Kippur War, Israel was attacked by Egypt, Syria, Iraq, and Jordan on the holiest day of the Jewish year. General Creighton Abrams, U.S. Army chief of staff, recommended a Ranger force be activated. These would be the first battalion-sized units since World War II. According to the army's Web site, www.goarmy.com, General Abrams wanted the unit to be "elite, light, and the most proficient infantry battalion in the world; a battalion that can do things with its hands and weapons better than anyone." As a result, the 75th Ranger Regiment was born. The 1st Battalion, 75th Infantry (Ranger) became effective January 24, 1974.

What Are the Benefits of Joining the Rangers?

Because the Ranger program is so competitive, the rewards are great. Rangers, like most Special Forces soldiers, feel a personal and professional satisfaction in being the best the American military has to offer. Others see the opportunity to be assigned overseas as a benefit. Many young Rangers look ahead and wonder what kind of job they will have once their military careers come to an end. These people may value the opportunity to master high-tech computer systems and receive language training.

Today's 75th Ranger Regiment is a highly skilled, rapidly deployable light infantry force. It can be anywhere in the world in eighteen hours or less. It can be used for many different objectives in a variety of environments. Today's Rangers are committed to excellence in combat performance. All are volunteers who must succeed in a very difficult and strenuous selection program before they become Rangers.

Soldiers who want to join the Rangers must meet a number of criteria. They must be active-duty male soldiers in one of a number of specific Military Occupational Specialties; be able to pass a secret clearance; be airborne qualified or willing to attend the U.S. Army Airborne School; and pass the Ranger Orientation Program/Ranger Assessment and Selection Program. (Lower ranking soldiers must pass the Ranger Indoctrination Program.)

U.S. Army 75th Ranger Regiment: Current Force Structure

The 75th Ranger Regiment is made up of the Ranger Regiment HQ (headquarters), located in Fort Benning, Georgia, and three battalions (the first in Hunter Army Airfield, Georgia; the second in Fort Lewis, Washington; and the third in Fort Benning). Each Ranger battalion consists of four companies: three combat companies and a battalion headquarters company. Each company is made up of four platoons: three rifle platoons and one weapons platoon. Training battalions are structured in the same way, but they are composed of rangers and officers-in-training.

Special Teams and Training

Rangers are often assigned to special teams, based on the needs of a mission. Many complete advanced special training in specific areas, such as those outlined below. Training is conducted in as many environments as possible. These environments include snow/mountains, jungle, desert, and water/land.

HALO Some missions call for high-altitude low-opening (HALO) parachute jumps. This technique requires the Ranger to jump out of a plane flying at a high altitude, and freefall for an extended period of time. This minimizes the chance that the Ranger is detected while being inserted into a hostile area. HALO team members must graduate from the Special Forces Freefall School.

HAHO Other missions call for high-altitude high-opening (HAHO) jumps. By employing this technique, a Ranger can "drift" in silence miles from the plane to his target. HAHO team members also graduate from the Special Forces Freefall School.

SCUBA Self-contained underwater breathing apparatus teams conduct special insertion and reconnaissance duties. Team members graduate from the Special Forces Underwater Operations School.

A Special Forces soldier practices a HALO parachute jump in the Philippines in training for rooting out terrorist cells abroad. The escalation in terrorist activities has forced the U.S. military to rely on stealth techniques to fight the enemy.

Scout swimmer   Scout swimmer teams conduct water operations in areas such as coastlines, swamps, and other inland waters. They participate in special insertion, reconnaissance, and security operations. Often they support Ranger amphibious operations. They use helicopters, scuba gear, and small watercraft. Scout swimmer team members are trained by landing-force training commands.

Demolition   Demolition teams are trained extensively in advanced demolition techniques with a variety of explosive devices and incendiaries. They are called into action for special operations as well as conventional operations.

By now you should have a pretty good idea just how special the U.S. Army Rangers are. As the armed forces' elite ground troops, they train hard to prepare for challenging physical tests. They study tactics and procedures and practice what they learn in open-field exercises. They master languages as well as weapons operations.

And you know how valuable the Rangers have been to this country and the world. Even before this land became the United States, through the American Revolution, the World Wars, and the more recent operations overseas, the Rangers have been here to lend their expertise and commitment to excellence. And they will continue to serve American military interests wherever and whenever they are needed.

Glossary

Allied forces European and American forces who united against the Axis powers of World War II.

amphibious Units capable of conducting operations from both the land and the water.

battalion A military unit consisting of a headquarters and two or more companies, batteries, or similar units.

cache A place used to hide supplies such as provisions and weapons.

company A unit of soldiers, often divided into smaller groups called platoons.

deploy To place military units in battle formation or in strategic locations.

exfiltration To exit a battle zone or hostile area.

guerrilla A soldier or unit who acts independently of a government to carry out sabotage or harassment.

infiltration   To pass troops individually or as units through gaps in enemy lines.

rappel   To descend a sheer, vertical surface using ropes.

reconnaissance   A military survey of enemy territory.

regiment   A military unit consisting of a number of battalions.

surveillance   Close watch over someone or something.

theater   A region where important military conflicts are resolved (as in "European theater").

tyranny   A government where a single individual has absolute power.

For More Information

United States Army
1500 Army Pentagon
Washington, DC 20310-1500
Web site: http://www.army.mil

U.S. Army Ranger Association
P.O. Box 52126
Fort Benning, GA 31995-2126
Web site: http://www.ranger.org

Web Sites

Due to the changing nature of Internet links, the Rosen Publishing Group, Inc., has developed an online list of Web sites related to the subject of this book. This site is updated regularly. Please use this link to access the list:

http://www.rosenlinks.com/iso/arra

For Further Reading

Koons, James. *The U.S. Army Rangers.* Mankato, MN: Capstone Press, 1995.

Landau, Alan M., and Frieda W. Landau. *Airborne Rangers.* New York: Barnes & Noble Books, 1999.

Lock, J. D. *The Coveted Black and Gold: A Daily Journey Through the U.S. Army Ranger School Experience.* Philadelphia: Xlibris Corporation, 2001.

Bibliography

ArmyRanger.com. Retrieved March 2002
  (http://www.armyranger.com).

Clancy, Tom, and John Gresham. *Special Forces: A Guided Tour of U.S. Army Special Forces*. New York: Berkley Books, 2001.

Clancy, Tom, and Tony Koltz. *Shadow Warriors: Inside the Special Forces*. New York: G. P. Putnam's Sons, 2002.

United States Army Infantry Home Page. "Ranger School Information." Retrieved March 2002 (http://www.benning. army.mil/rtb).

United States Army Ranger Association Web site. Retrieved March 2002 (http://www.ranger.org).

United States Army Web site. Retrieved April 2002 (http:// www.goarmy.com).

Waller, Douglas C. *The Commandos: The Inside Story of America's Secret Soldiers*. New York: Simon & Schuster, 1994.

Index

About the Author

J. Poolos is a freelance writer who lives in Iowa City, Iowa.

Acknowledgement

The author wishes to give special thanks to Joseph Brizz.

Credits

Cover, p. 1 © AFP/Corbis; pp. 4, 26, 27, 37, 41 © Corbis; pp. 9, 13 © Hulton/Archive/Getty Images; p. 11 © Medford Historical Society Collection/Corbis; pp. 12, 30, 49, 55 © AP/Wide World Photos; pp. 15, 18, 22, 44 © Bettmann/ Corbis; p. 31 © Annie Griffiths Belt/Corbis; pp. 38, 42 © Military Stock Photo.

Editor

Christine Poolos

Design and Layout

Les Kanturek